CW01023253

Field Recordings: BBC Poems (1998-2008)

Paul Farley was born in Liverpool and now lives in north Lancashire. He received the Somerset Maugham Award and a Forward Prize for his first collection of poems, and was Sunday Times Young Writer of the Year in 1999. His second collection, *The Ice Age*, won the Whitbread Poetry Award, while his third, *Tramp in Flames*, was shortlisted for the Forward, Griffin and T.S. Eliot prizes. In 2009 he received the E.M. Forster Award from the American Academy of Arts and Letters.

Also by Paul Farley

The Boy from the Chemist is Here to See You (Picador)
The Ice Age (Picador)
Tramp in Flames (Picador)
Distant Voices, Still Lives (BFI Publishing)
John Clare (Faber and Faber Poet to Poet series)

Field Recordings: BBC Poems (1998-2008)

Paul Farley

Donut Press

Published by Donut Press in 2009.

Donut Press, PO Box 45093,
London, N4 1UZ.
www.donutpress.co.uk

Printed and bound by
The Colourhouse,
Arklow Road Trading Estate, Arklow Road,
London, SE14 6EB.

Donut Press gratefully acknowledges
the support of Arts Council England.

ISBN: 9780955360466

A CIP record for this book is available
from the British Library.

LOTTERY FUNDED

For the Producers

Acknowledgements

Many thanks to all the producers and editors at the BBC who've encouraged me to write something for the wireless over the past decade, particularly Tim Dee, Zahid Warley, Allegra McIlroy, Emma Harding, Susan Roberts, Julian May, Mohit Bakaya, Nicola Holloway, Fiona McLean, Ekene Akalawu, Clare Holland, Martin Smith, Aasiya Lodhi, Ella-Mai Robey and especially Robert Ketteridge, who was the first producer to risk giving me airtime. I should also thank Ben Smith and Mikis Michaelides, Maddy Paxman, Karen Lockney, Carole Romaya and Julian Turner; and a radiophonic shout goes out to Andy Ching in Haringey for his unfailing support and persistence with this project.

P.F.

'An Erratic' and 'Diary Moon' first appeared in *The Ice Age* (Picador, 2002); 'The Big Hum' and 'Civic' appeared in *Tramp in Flames* (Picador, 2006). Donut Press would like to thank Picador for their co-operation regarding the inclusion of the above poems.

Contents

Field Recordings: BBC Poems (1998-2008)

The Sorting Office

We were, although we couldn't know it then,
like castaways, like cold-ocean captains
who make a postman of an albatross:
a leathern tally round its neck, the compass
mark and ship's time sent into the night.
Our own requests were every bit as desperate.
One year I counted maps, a Timex wrist-
watch, and a telescope on my wish list;
another, snowfall on the stroke of midnight
in blank verse it took me hours to write.

You could say that those birds' notes, meant for man,
were taken from their charges in heaven.
You could say that. Or you could say behind
that Greenland address you'd only find
a team of seasonal temps, a wheelbarrow,
an oil-drum brazier burning in the snow
where raked embers are sending chinks and sparks
back on their way to join the winter stars.

Chalk: an Epistle

I'm writing from a box bedroom of childhood,
breeze-blocked on some lost night. If I wrote 'Rain
moving in from the west' or 'Irish Sea: good'
you'd catch my damp drift, could easily clone
the sea wall I slept next to, the escarpment
wind that rakes the landing, lifting up
the letterbox. Ideas become fitments
and before you know there is a northern landscape
and me inside a lit window within it,
cosily setting down this black wet idyll,
the whole thing up and running in a minute,
a second. Let me stop you in the middle:

I'm only interested in chalk. I've had enough
of what surrounds me. If this is to work
imagine how, today, I've pulled the legs off
creatures, spat and been spat on, got kicks
from setting fire to things, and in the cruel light
of my imagination and a bedside
lamp, I've opened up a book to write
myself out of the day, dusting its blackboards
down. So, clean and blank, I start again
using my library of Ladybirds.

I'm writing this for you in one of their flyleaves,
the only kid around here who believes
these full-colour illustrations of the South.
Bright red post vans climbing from village mists,
look-outs calculating the curve of the earth
from cliff-tops, spying as a clipper's masts

sail beyond the publisher's remit: *What to Look For in Spring*
means what grows in, or turns up on, British soil.
I've scoured the days and never found a thing
but read these books in bed and pray it's all
happening elsewhere. Did those illustrators
have any idea that they inspired
such devotions in the North? Am I a traitor
for harbouring such thoughts? Either way, I've wired
a landscape up: the picture books have brought
the same faithful construction work to mind,
the sunken lanes, dusty and white, have caught
their corridors of day-heat; rivers wind
their way slowly to sea, rivers with names
from maps – Adur, Arun – which I can stock
and fringe carefully with other names which come
from the Observer's books. I know it like
the scaled down universe of the hobbyist
who walks giant-like between papier-mâché hills;
as intimately as a shower or sea mist
will feel its way inland. I dwell in details
and learn how words can be things in themselves:
these maps that haven't seen service outdoors
have place names stepping out beyond the shelve
of beaches, into the blue, like little piers,
and on the spoiler of a Brighton train
I hurl in sped-up footage for this coast,
from the clinker of Victoria, through the grain
of fifty miles of bramble, to the last
great buffers, with the sea at the end of the road,
where 'Brighton' is the word 'Britain' switched on,

every day is Whit Monday and I'm a Mod
being baton-charged along the shingle. Then

putting out the light, my fringed lampshade
leaves the after-image of a jellyfish,
and I'm plunged into a warm sea without words,
and let the prehistorical saline wash
the wounds clean. After all this rushing about
my frame of reference is barely a film
a molecule thick, picked up by slant sunlight.
The Chalk-hill blues flittering between Latin names
are doing so on an eternity's skin,
a mass, unnumbered burial at sea,
a steady marine snowfall; skeletons
of creatures off the end of a pin, algae
who had their lives to lead as we do now.
The surface scratched, the bone pile underneath
revealed, you'd think might lead to nightmares, though
suspension in the fluids before Truth
and Faith and Valour is strangely comforting.

And so I'd wipe my slate and sink to sleep
each night by carefully imagining
a chalkscape. I see no reason to keep
to this story of me writing from a room
in childhood: over thirty million years
of mindless building work and one mad zoom
at the end, a couple of decades here and there
will make so little difference as to mean
sweet nothing. And I have lived on chalk for a year

at the end of the millennium: summer storms
stacked up over the Channel, the West Pier
still in its slow collapsing fade, great swarms
of birds like northern lights in negative
trawling for home, that bookshop's big window
with millions of closed pages on the move,
all intricate, unreadable, vast and slow.

Sea floors, water levels, old horizons …
Is there some vestige of a memory
which made me feel nostalgic for the Downs
and Weald before I'd been there? Did I see,
beyond the bright green hills, the washed blue skies
of books, the solving undercoat of chalk
as paradise? This picture book disguise
which took me in had shallow seas like milk
beneath it, all the time, a nourishment
tapped into after rain-dark sandstone hours.
And whether this lies in my bones, or is heaven sent,
my mind, idle, at rest, always goes there.

North Atlantic Corridor

Halfway, it's noisier than you'd expect.
A wind-up gramophone is playing Caruso
in a U-boat underneath a convoy lane,
whose crew can testify to whale song,

and most have heard the eels and salmon pass
on moonlit nights, when the click of binary
cabling the ocean floor is deafening,
and the elements compete above the swell

where the tern's wave-top flight path intersects
with ragtime from a glittering liner,
where woodworm in the Old World's darkwood hold
meets the tongues of RKO and MGM

and there's no peace, even at altitude:
halfway between London and New York
an in-flight movie can't make up its mind:
A Matter of Life and Death/Stairway to Heaven.

The Spindle

On wet nights, under broad Atlantic fronts,
the country is a plate of ancient shellac
a Troll slips from its sleeve and holds up squint
to the moon. He grimaces at all the cracks

then blows on it – the first true autumn storm –
and puts it on the continental platter.
The compass rumbles round. He lifts the arm
across and settles down. The wow and flutter

of Bailey, Fair Isle, Forties fills his hall,
and every lighthouse spins at thirty-three.
Trolls like a steady hiss, backwash and calm,
a needle ploughing through a mindless sea;

a penny from the Kingdom of the Trolls
(an ugly coinage still in tender, struck
from dross, showing the Queen in zero profile)
steadies the needle on its lonely track

then with a sonar pop it hits Rockall
and trails diminuendoed dolphin clicks.
The Troll sits up. He knows a big landfall
of sound – the geological re-mix –

will hit the beach – he's played this one before –
but nothing can prepare you for the grind
of pure granitic schist, the shock and awe
of Cornish death metal, the constant pound

of Connaught's gneiss. It *is* a bitching groove
the Troll thinks, on his feet now, getting down
to some serious head-banging, making his moves,
before the track picks up the bumps and grain

of softer shires, the business corridors
where tinny solos make their presence felt.
Above the beat, the Troll practises air guitar.
The needle fords the rivers, jumps the faults,

then locks into a rut where the human world
is a plain of dates and laws, logos and language.
The Troll can go no further. Suddenly old
and frail, he stands watch on the crackly edge

and listens to the hum of a bad earth.
The autumn stars turn on heavy rotation.
Polaris climbs the sky. The Troll heads north
because time is running down. In every version

the fluff he chased and the coin he used for ballast
turn into other things – hill snow, great boulders –
and the land is slipped inside its sleeve of frost,
and for a while the world lies still, and colder.

The Sound of Music

Sometimes I catch myself whistling a tune
and am shocked to find it's from *The Sound of Music*:
which went to Number One in early June
the summer I was born. I'm told the basic
beat my tapping foot always defaults to
is the Supremes' 'Stop in the Name of Love';
and I've always had this thing for 'Homesick Blues'.
I say *always*, but mean more. I believe
I tuned into our wireless from the womb,
late term, when my feathery fingers had hardened
enough to click in time, and my eardrum
could pick the difference up between each band.
Foetal fans of The Beatles and The Stones!
We spill over, backwards into that other
floating world; could feel in soft bones
the throb of Motown, croon of The Searchers.
Wired to my mother, every track
she turned up sank in deep, for all I know.
She was sitting down for tea when her waters broke,
right in the middle of *Ready Steady Go!*

Ports

I

I want you to imagine, in your late capitalist's mind's eye,
a stagnant fly-blown lake under an African sun,
the smell of the sea just beyond (this at least should come easy
being the universal saltwater of all of your childhoods).
Armies of ants on parade in the poor weeds and grey sludge
of the ages, dismantling the scene in their own time-lapse movie,
skeletal cats picking over the spoil, boneyard mongrels
marking their range by the water's edge before moving on.
I want you to imagine all this, because once I was Carthage
and still am in name, though like some poisoned inland sea
my horizons have shrunk to a port that handles zero tonnage,
an import and export that evens the scales up at nil,
not counting the old rope and plastic bottles that come knocking
with the tides, not counting the rusted tins that drift in,
not counting the ants shifting clay forms and Carrera marble
from my ruins, or the guide who conducts his own private dig
for unscrupulous tourists who think nothing of removing
a coin from its context (if money ever has such set contexts),
of taking a Roman penny with an obverse of Augustus
out of the country, to reach the cold northern latitudes
in the holds of Lufthansa or Aeroflot, in a fraction
of the time it once took under oar and Ursa Major.
I was Carthage, but nothing much comes or goes in this afterwards;
all that's left of a thousand years of dockyards and shipsheds
are a few shapes the soft earth has found indigestible,
for the tourist to squint at, consider, weigh up, reconstruct
imaginatively, as I am asking you, listener.
From this silted salt lake I once pulled the strings of the known world.

Lovers looked out from my sea walls into a powerful distance
that bound them in knowing that I was a true centre.
They pulled tight their merchant purses. They drank from clay pitchers –
under glass now in nearby museums. A museum will go some way
to help in your excavations, but what stories lead on from
the razors and combs and amphora and ostrich egg masks
are the details of millions who passed through, then into the ground.
Standing over a scale model in its sea of flat glass
acts out a dominion of your time over mine, looking down on
my circular dockyard apotheosis; looking down
as from a great height, in a way I can never have known.
A map might be easier in helping you build on my wasteland:
my trade routes once lit up the coastlines in thousands of oil lamps,
a Phoenician outline of Africa in the antique night,
spreading westward and hugging the shore, a luminous tracing
that brought in and foundered sea creatures, signalling for their mates.
I can still taste the distant metals like blood in my harbour mouth,
the tin and the iron and the copper which don't come here now
but leech down the well-furrowed sea lanes, my phantom nerve endings.
Carthaginian and Roman and Vandal are blinks in my brine eye,
in each of their own eternities: to me they rise and fall
as sea swell. Credit me, listener, with such a long memory,
as more than the sum of my parts, more than archaeology
and soft sump, more than ground fought over. Aeneas stood here once
with a mind to call it quits and cut loose, so the story goes,
my port in his storm to his girl in every port.
The jets tilt and bank heading north for their carrier hubs
in Frankfurt and Moscow, without so much as a second thought
for me in my modern darkness, their starboard wing lights
blinking in an element I knew nothing about.

Some things have endured: the peaks of Cap Bon across the bay
form a backdrop to nothing much doing these days; the stars rise
to guide nobody from my mouth and on course for the Pillars
of Hercules – but these things give me a sense of myself,
as the winds do, strong at the turns in the year, which remind me
of cargoes and freights in their seasons, gross tonnes that passed through
as sand through an hour glass, until history,
like the idea of magnetic north so long in the discovering,
moved slowly away from here, like a great ship embarking
out onto the future's broad main, and this is the fate
of all ports, even yours, listener. Listen to me. I was Carthage.

II

They left by the back door, caught the first train
for Euston, they watched the city pull away
and open country take its place; they left
by bus and charabanc, by motorway
that began anonymously then rose on pillars
to meet my boundary; they left in droves
or dribs and drabs, and if they hadn't shown
as planned, their so-called friends went on without them;
they left by any means, stowing away
in First Class toilets or under tarpaulin
on big artics; they left without paying the bill
and did a runner for the rest of their lives;
they left like silent cinema, in twos
by moonlit rail, see-sawing up and down;
they left like Beatlemania and pulled their hair;
they left in such a hurry kettles stood warm

on stoves: they left behind such textbook clues;
they left on jet planes and they didn't know
when they'd be back again, like in the song;
they left like in the Book of Exodus
or were just going outside, and may be some time;
they left me looking like the Marie Celeste;
they left by side entrance, they left scraping
the manhole covers back above their heads
or pulling up a rope of sheets; they left
without so much as a goodbye or a kiss my arse;
they left on eggshells, closed doors quietly
behind them, or they threw the kinds of parties
where washbasins get ripped off walls; they left
behind important legacies, their names,
or nothing but a nasty smell; they left
in floods of tears or couldn't wait to see
the back of me; they left the day the word
'city' became standard instead of 'port';
they left in the clothes they were standing up in;
they left, but it was alright, they'd be back;
they left knowing there was no going back
even though 'the door is always open'; they left
because the engine of the world was running
outside; they left to serve apprenticeships
or marry badly; they left to serve some time
and, liking what they saw, they left again;
they left, and a mighty wind blew in their wakes,
or a litter devil span along a street;
they left, and it was called a haemorrhage
by a spokesman for the Office of National Statistics;

they left, and what am I, some kind of mug
who's tattooed with a giant exit sign?;
they left and spat, or left so effortlessly
they didn't know they were leaving, and wouldn't see
the likes of me again; they left early
and said 'we're leaving early'; they left to feed
the brain drain and the casual labour market;
they left, and didn't have a decent word
to say about me in their new worlds
with big skies and four clearly defined seasons;
they left because Australia needed them
and they were overqualified; they left
because they might as well, just for the hell of it,
because everybody else was doing it;
they left without a hope, full of high hopes;
they left and then regretted it with anyone
they met; they left and sung about the leaving
in bars across the world; they left big buildings
looking stupid in the gorgeous light
they'd left; they left thousands of square feet
of empty warehouse space for rats and mice
to occupy in the dark years; they left
under a cloud; they left and earned the keys
to the city or were given pauper's funerals;
they left and the whole street came out, or no-one
cared; they left under their own steam,
and I'll tell you this for nothing: they left, but none
of them who did the leaving left by sea.

III

Rotterdam calling. City of light.
North Sea traffic. Candlepower.
No time to reflect. I work all night.
Straight to the point. Container port.
Almighty hub. Words fail me, so
I speak in code: the radar blip
and flag flown do the biz. Can't stop.
There's barges in and barges out
around the clock. Containers are
your building blocks, my skyline, our
Boxopolis that tessellates
and hardly makes the same shape twice.
City of light. What's in the box?
I knew you'd ask. Just look around
the room you're in, listening to this:
half of it's been through Rotterdam.
Shirt on your back, shoes on your feet,
dinner in your oven, oven in your kitchen,
the plugs in your ear, the air freshener
barnacled to your dash, the petrol
in your tank, the watch you wind
or lift to your eyes' horizon line,
the lead in your pencil, the sizzle in your sausage,
and, of course, this radio you've tuned in.
At some point back along the line
I've said hello and goodbye to them all
and will see them again, in another form.
I contain the dreaming western world

remaking and remodelling itself.
Look at the building blocks themselves:
a sea container falls into place
with a hollow sound like nothing else,
and they rise in abstract avenues
eight deep in places, labyrinthine
enough to require an A-Z,
strange greens and reds: the marine palette
you'll find is the exact opposite
of domestic space, but fashion sense
is far from my mind. These are the colours
of banknotes, of making yourself understood.
Words give no clues to what's inside:
Genstar, UBC, Seaco,
and Dream Box (which is a favourite of mine)
given how the leaden light of day
never inundates, so the light of the mind
can be given play, though idle souls
in fluorescent jerkins and overalls
are rare in docks busy as a hive
in spring. The words will give no clues
though some shipments advertise themselves
to the nose: wandering a terminal
can be like walking through a Javanese wood
turned geometric under a Dutch sky;
the pepper notes float out of place,
the ghost of somewhere far away.
This is as nostalgic as it gets.
(OK. I will allow one display
case of knots in the Maritime Hotel.)

We have no old rope. We have no bananas.
We have no classical tropes. Or if
we do, they are all safely boxed up,
all the same to the mighty grabbing device,
to the quarter kilometre barge.
City of light. On the captain's face
sat before the radar binnacle,
a greenish glow. On the civic bridge
a blade of halogen. On the trucks
festooned in it that come and go.
And will I dim? Experts predict
only a general brightening,
and so the decadent poets wait
off in the future, or watch the boats
for now, while it's all still happening,
and wonder why they love their names,
and build things in their dark bow wakes
that go like this: *Marlene Green*,
Atlantic Trader, *Flinterstar*,
Antilles Janet, *Heading Home*,
Iver Expert, *Galaxy*,
Innuendo, *Arklow Sally*,
Sayonara, *C'est la Vie …*

IV

Ports rise and fall. The stars climb from the eastern sea.
The balance sheets all even out. The sand wipes clean.
Nobody comes here now except to dig deep down.
The nights are still and dark. There is no sound

beyond the constant waves' profit and loss sheets.
I was Carthage, tall and handsome as any city,
but the world has passed me by. The maps have been redrawn
and you can see how it might have been for Dido,
left standing while her life shipped out, moved on for home;
which sailors know lies off ahead and elsewhere.
The earth seems scorching to their feet. This will last forever,
or as long as there are seas and men to sail them.
But I was Carthage, tall and handsome. Remember my name.

For St Jerome

(*Librarians*)

Guardian of the date-stamp and card catalogue,
keeper of knowledge, and a staff notice-board
pinned with drunks and men who lick the atlases,
go with me while I Tipp-Ex-out the bogies
and spray Glade in the newspaper section.
Curmudgeon, teach me how to smile while fining
the sinners who have lately been in hospital,
who were struck dumb by lightning, or forgot.
Teach me to bear their crumbs and bookmarks
with the fortitude for which you are not famous:
the bus tickets, postcards, rashers of bacon
and once – give me strength – a knotted condom.
Gatekeeper, watch over books on loan;
their months of purgatory spent in bath steam
or under beds. Watch over those abandoned
on bus seats or park benches. Heal the torn.
Take them back from houses with the measles.
Inform Environmental Health at once.
And teach me to work with an abrupt demeanour,
the martyrdom of the index, which was yours;
to speak out in the silence of your feast day
whose widespread celebration is long overdue.

An Erratic

This glacial boulder weighs nearly a ton.
Its parent group is Cumberland volcanic.
After aeons it was moved by sheet ice
to the Mersey basin. In 1908
the City Engineer placed it here
in front of Wavertree District Library,
behind these black railings, a 'meteorite'
to generations of schoolchildren since.
Some still run their fingers round its surface
but its work here is done: any magnetic
properties have dimmed with age, and so
it essays now on scruple and endurance.
Somewhere inside the lending library
you'll find it mentioned by George Harrison
in his book I Me Mine *(where he also*
praises the quality of Liverpool water,
as fine as any he'd known for washing hair,
so altering the course of popular culture).

Blind Scouse

Great Stews of the World makes no mention
of standard scouse, nor its runnier cousin
made minus even scrag-end of lamb.
Recession food. Root vegetables and shame.

An International Cuisine of Thrift
claims comprehensiveness, but doesn't list
blind scouse among the gumbos and run-downs;
between 'beetrootless borscht' and 'bloodless bourguignon'.

Cooking with all the Senses shouldn't include
blind scouse, it being one sense short; indeed
two if we take taste into account,
and checking the index, I'm glad to see it doesn't.

So blind scouse slips from view, falls off the map,
out of the literature. I doubt a single pan
is being prepared tonight from the blank verse
of a carrot and two spuds, for better or for worse.

In Liftless Country

Bored by the hills, we bored into them.
I invented a lift that fell from Helvellyn's
airy penthouse, through a secret door

set back into a cairn – three thousand feet
in seconds – then a long stone corridor
out through its base; imagined dark Skiddaw

as a cutaway Valley of the Kings
diagram revealing shafts and vents;
descended in those doorless, wardrobe cars

found in cheap Parisian hotels,
dropping through the Ordovician floors –
slate, shale, grit, volcanic chert ...

while you took an express and waited for me
in the mountain's mezzanine. And so we'd meet
in a granite atrium, or lower down

in a room of broken photocopiers
and mop buckets: a couple skiving off
for a smoke, tired of walking in the clouds.

Movers and Shakers

I'm networking my arse off in the sticks.
I'm new, so need to put myself about.
Sunrise, a good walk up the Coffin Path
where I meet the wren, the jay, the shy dunnock,
who are nice as pie. We swapped names and addresses
and said we must do this again. Lunchtime
on the riverbank, and I know I'll get noticed
at this seat, where the char's refracted gaze
regards me. I can feel their big Atlantic
connections, that muscle tone that sends
the small fry to the reed beds as one man.
I catch sight of the frog who eats here,
can hear the bleeps and purrs of big business.
I'm still on a different time: my body clock
is tuned into the rhythms of the street
but I'm getting there. The afternoon wears on
and it's not that different from Soho or Fitzrovia;
a bunch of swallows on expense accounts
are still at it. The buzzard is back at work
setting a slower tone, the post-lunch fug
where everything winds down on warm thermals
and we move into evening, which is busy here
as well. Tonight, I'll dine among the trees,
those big gossips, who'll whisper to each other
and never let me in on anything.

Shitemere

It rains all the time: let's get that one out of the way.
So: this is the county of carrier bags,
of 'Bags for Life', of bags worn over the head
or tied above those sensible shoes you brought.
The county where you 'step in and look around'
jigsaw emporia, ten thousand piecers
of lake surfaces for those special washouts;
stinky charity shops, Teasmades and 'What To Do
Here When it Rains, 1979',
and all that camping equipment someone must
be using, somewhere … The lakes are shallow as England
and stringy with what they said was *lollo rosso*
or *cavalo nero* where you ate last night.
Remember how you held your drink to the light?
You were a traveller then, steaming
by the horse brasses, now you are a tourist
again. A yard of doggerel was written.
The strangled cries of writers-in-residence
travel for miles on the damp air. Stick to the roads.
Jenners proudly announce their new seasonal ale.
It's just as tiring going downhill as uphill
in Shitemere, everybody will tell you so.
There is an etiquette of the hills to be observed,
though don't speak to him, he's entered a vow of silence
for a week: a hermit funded by the Arts Council.
No more questions now, please. The photo editor
has all he needs to select the sourest shot.
Umbrellas of the Premiership, salt and vinegar
in sachets: blimey, we must still be in Shitemere.

Civic

Somebody should write on the paranoia of pines
  I wonder, making my way down to the shore
    of the reservoir in the dark,
      ignoring the signs
    which warn of deep water;
  there's a spring underfoot made up
of a billion needles and cones that carpet the floor

and a criss-cross of roots that keep the earth in its place
  and so the water clear: I've read the reports
    of the city engineers, done my homework,
      and move through the woods
    warily, the canopy high above
  whispering, watching (though I'm about as far
from another human being as it's possible to get

here; from our cities where you're never more than a few feet
  from a rat; where cameras comb the streets
    all hours), looking over my shoulder
      and seeing myself
    like that footage of sasquatch;
  or the private eye in *Chinatown*, hired
in a drought to find out what's happened to all the water

when all at once it's before me, a great glassy sheet,
  dark trees and hillsides held upside down
    in starlight: I've found Manchester
      at source, in the blues
    of a bathymetric map, in the clean
  and still repose before the nightmare of taps
and kettles. I scoop a cold handful up to my mouth

and taste the great nothing that comes before pipes
  pass on their trace of lead, before fonts
    leech their peck of limestone,
     before public baths
    annihilate with chlorine.
  The mind, honeycombed with aquaducts,
is lapping on the walls of Nineveh or Imperial Rome

but this is where it begins, if we can describe
  water in such terms, with middles and ends.
    I can hear the sluices – sound
      carries at this hour –
    and the start of the journey
  down, to the distant city, a steady roar
acting as water's own bar pilot, river guide, exit sign

and gravity holds open the door onto a man-made dark,
  culverts at first, and then the all enclosing
    mysteries of pipework;
      a gentle incline
    and two miles-per-hour
  average flow through the fell, blind
though sometimes proud when bridging a beck or ghyll

aloofly, sealed in concrete, on official council business.
  Two miles-per-hour; a hundred miles,
    so by my reckoning it'll take
      just over two days:
    if there was anybody else
  up here with me, I'd suggest 'Pooh sticks'
played out on a glacial, OS Pathfinder scale

or introduce those bright dyes I've seen used in the field
  in this very catchment area, turning streams
    a turbulent day-glo in a matter
      of stopwatched minutes;
    then catch a bus or train in my own time
  down to the city, and wait in the Albert Square
for the fountain to turn orangeade, cream soda or dandelion

and burdock. You could walk: no Roman would have given
  a second thought to the hike, no Romantic neither.
    But this is water's pause for reflection.
      This is its downtime.
    Water the asylum seeker
  lying low for a while, taking a chance
to gather its thoughts. Years ago, in the Liverpool Aquarium,

I read how the lungfish would dig into the parched
  riverbed, curl into a ball, secrete
    mucous, and generally do
      what it needed to
    to weather a spell between
  broad sheets of sudden rainfall that fell
weeks or months or years apart, wrapped up in itself;

though there was no word next to the tank on how water too
  needs to introspect, to find some high cistern
    or a road's camber after a storm
      that can hold a moon;
    those baths you see in fields
  plumbed into whitethorn, where the Green Man
might take his murky ablutions before going to ground

are favourites too. Wind from out of nowhere disturbs
the signal. Some of these trees are mobile masts
disguised as trees, I'm told, and this
lake a reservoir
disguised as a lake. It looks
the part alright; in fact, has already starred
in films as body double to Como and Geneva

though it knows it's an offcomer, a baby in glacial terms,
and nothing much has pooled and stuck. There's no
host of golden daffodils, no
Bluebird going down
in black and white to rise
again in colour, no Post Office Tower
leant like a dipstick to illustrate its unnatural fathoms,

just those rumours that seem to follow reservoirs around:
a drowned village, church bells on rough nights,
the souls who stood their ground
calling from the depths,
that kind of thing. Then a blackbird
breaks cover, and its cries manage to sound
genuinely bereft for lost acres of thicket and undergrowth

and miles of hedgerow. A Water Board van snakes its way
silently northwards up the A591
along the opposite bank,
and it's getting light
so I step back into the trees
not wanting to be seen by anyone.
In this poem disguised as a meditation on water

it's now as good a time as any to tell you, listener,
how I've driven up to this spot in a hire car
and stand at the water's edge
drawn by a keen sense
of civic duty: I plan to break
the great stillness and surface of this lake-
cum-reservoir by peeing quietly into the supply

and no harm will come to anything or anyone. Consider
this: no shoal will surface out of sync
like driftwood; no citizens
will draw a cold draft
of LSD, or run a hot bath
of nerve agent in two day's time. This protest
is so small it will only really occur in the mind's eye

and those particles – smaller than rods and cones – that escape
  the filters and treatment plant won't register
    in any sense. And so my ripples
      head for God-knows-where
    as light strengthens by increment
  and a tree falls in the woods and no-one hears,
though I can't swear to any of this: I wasn't here.

Somebody else packed up in a hurry, walked back
  up a slope, bastard tricky with roots, came to
    the quiet road in the green shade
      that leads round the lake;
    passed a city's coat of arms
  and some Latin he couldn't read, looked out
from a wall across a body of water at chest height

and gasped at the thought of the pressure, the pounds-per-brick,
  and felt alone up there then, and wanted to drive
    far away from those high offices,
      from the danger signs
    where water stands in the hills
  with the eyes, from the man-made distances
that have haunted his ears; from the paranoia of pines.

She Wandered

'Daffodils' was drilled into young heads
sat serried two-to-a-desk, written via chalk
on slate, and etched into the wet dark beds
of tissue, cut and laid down like a track

in bakelite, in snowy fats. The cane
cracked down on any desk lid occupied
by pupils gazing through the windowpane
onto the smoke-field, brick-filled view outside

and so it all went in one ear and *stayed*
because its flight would mean being kept behind,
or worse. Classrooms the length of the land obeyed
and in this way a generation learned.

They carry it around, though you'd have to search
past lumbered playground names and early curses,
through stockrooms full of things boomed out in church,
silence at tables, or the Home Service,

and there, like mangles or carborundum stones,
you'll find it, stored away inside this era,
intact but out of mind, a poem's bones
slipped down into the backs of settees, drawers,

until an unlooked-for points-flash of syntax –
in a form for housing benefit or a line
on a hoarding – has some stop dead in their tracks
to mouth: *Continuous as the stars that shine …*

and, despite the funny looks, they smile inwardly
remembering their desk-mate and the chant
as they push a pram to the shops; others hardly
register, ordering another pint,

but even though nothing's happening, and the poem
has sunk like rain into a wall, has passed
into a night safe silence within them,
one thing remains certain: it's never lost,

of this I'm sure because, as they're washed away
to dentures and gallstones, it keeps its shape
and can be found recited in the day-
centres and care homes: as their world breaks up

like snow spawning in sodium lamps, as sheets
are drawn across street furniture, I heard
one woman with eyes as dark as inkwells light
upon its ancient fixed wreckage: *I wandered …*

A Stranger's Guide

He jumped ship. The story could have ended there.
He could have met a girl on Paradise Street
or fallen for the sunsets you get here.
Finding the *Pocket Companion* to this port

useless, he could have set about his own;
become a writer of sorts, and tapped
into a talent he'd never known.
He could have kept up with new docks

and boarded-up hotels, weaving his prose
from place of interest to curiosity
and made a good living each time he froze
a new version of this city,

even enjoyed seeing his older works
drift slowly into nostalgia,
the honeycombed alleyways and walks
broadening into gaslight, each miniature

of slum and civic life: pipesmoke, the tap
of canes, shouts in the night. But sometimes
the river at the end of a street would snap
a watery bright message back at him,

and he'd get that feeling – it always passed
quickly, though there were times when he was found
in tears – that feeling that he was lost
and something huge was following him around.

Synchronous Lateral Excitation

You're neither here nor there, one or the other.
You've stepped aboard. You've joined a human river.
You've walked into the open and real weather.
You'll cross this blade, but it will take forever.

Saint Paul's seems to begin in these first steps.
The Bankside, Tate and Globe return your stare.
This is as silent as the city gets.
Has Southwark anything to show more fair?

The river asks us moon and tide questions.
Perhaps you catch the gentlest hint of sway.
A wind blows from the west. You think of oceans.
It's not the wind that makes it move this way.

What if everyone were thinking this same thought?
What if all of Britain locked in pace?
The day has held its breath. You feel your heart.
Stop. Break step. Your hands go to your face.

Then someone calls the *Standard* and it lifts.
Something moved you. Was it grace or fear?
The buildings stand there like the lives we've left.
The bank you've reached is neither there nor here.

July (Wedding Haiku)

The ladybird's wing
trails from its shell: a bride's dress
caught in the car door.

The Great Violinski

Violinski, great composer, mighty renderer
of thunder, lightning, *sturm und drang*, your music
has travelled far since your untimely death:
I've even been stopped on council estates
and asked: 'Is that the new Violinski CD?'

And you were deaf! Deaf as a post while scoring
an opus. Though the individual names
of your works escape us, we know them fugitively
when whistled or incidental. O Violinski,
why were you such an influence on the Nazis?

Knocking out quintets in the grip of syphilis;
the penury; the slide into the limepit.
Somewhere in Mittel Europa there must be
a visitor centre, stretched and under-funded,
preparing for the anniversary:

they plan to send fireworks into the night,
to play your music drifting down a river.
There should be free concerts in the parks
of all the major cities. The Three Tenors
should sing your choral masterpiece, Violinski:

the one about the girl in the match factory.
The wavebands should be radiant in your memory.
Applause should drift out through the fire exits
this August night, like smoke into the city;
then silence should resume and leave us lonely.

World of Sport

Munich Olympics, 1972

Everybody thought they were Mark Spitz
that summer in the Picton Road Public Baths
and I went to great lengths to get the badge
for treading water for a full two minutes,
for swimming underwater for a width,
and diving in the deep end for a rubber brick.

It was easy to fall in love with Olga Korbut
at seven, because, in a world of Chinese burns,
dead legs and monkey grips and camel bites;
in a world of split kippers and being the Third
Wise Man, of going over handlebars
and getting drivers of the charabanc
to pull up and being sick on the hard shoulder;
in a world of greenstick fractures and the smash
of glass always, somewhere off in the night,
Olga had balance.

The Grand National, Aintree, 1973

Crisp tires at The Elbow. Red Rum closes
the gap from fifteen lengths. I'm in a house
near Aintree, and my aunt has turned the sound down
so we can hear the hoofbeats of the horses.

World Heavyweight Championship Fight, Zaire, 1974

Cock of the Infants, Cock of the Juniors,
he came to the end of his reign one four-
o'clock by the gates of the top playground.
I was in the crowd that gathered round
and like Norman Mailer said later
in the same time zone, on the Equator,
the winner's arm was ready and cocked
for a punch he didn't need to land,
when the school was dark and the gates padlocked.

European Cup Final, Rome, 1977

As Tommy Smith – the 'Anfield Iron' – heads in from off a corner
the meter goes and in the dark we scream for shillings and tanners.

The Ashes, Headingley, 1981

If I say it was a summer full of cider
and Test Match Special on the radio
it sounds idyllic, but there was a wider
world now and I knew that Ground Zero
lay just five miles away, and every night
brought an imagined blast and boundaries.
I used to count the rings and hope the light
would be the first and last thing I would see.

Men's Singles Final, Wimbledon, 1985

We're turning down the sound again.
Centre Court is just a page
away in the London A-Z,
so Concorde on its long descent
is heard twice – in the shiny world
onscreen, then in the other world
we live in – at the same time
as Boris Becker, at seventeen,
is ushering in the modern game.

World Snooker Championship Final, Sheffield, 1986

Snooker on a black and white portable
taught me how to see colours in greyscale.
The 'black ball fight' happened in the early hours
and, far from home, I thought of how my father
loved to snooze before a frame of snooker,
his chin, on cue, dropping; his bifocals
skew-whiff on his nose like Dennis Taylor's.

World Cup Semi-Final, Turin, 1990

In a big year for tears –
at Number Ten and on a pitch
in Italy – we were in floods
of our own, in private, everywhere.
Oh yes. And wouldn't you like to know.

Winter Olympic Games, Salt Lake City, 2002

The way those women polish the ice clean
isn't so much Bill Brandt's sad step scrubber
but the frantic housewives wired on Dexedrine
whose curlers I can just about remember.

Diary Moon

You are the plainest moon. Forget all others
shivering in pools or spoken to when drunk,
that great Romantic gaze of youth. Shed all
sonatas, harvests, Junes, and think instead
of how your pages turn here in a diary:
stripped of sunlight, surface noise and seas,
you move unnoticed through the months, a bare limn
achieving ink blackness, emptying again.

You who turned inside the week-to-view
my father carried round each day, past crosses
that symbolised pay days, final demands;
in girlfriends', where red novae marked the dates
they were 'due on', and I shouldn't've been looking;
who even showed in weighty Filofaxes,
peeping through the clouds of missed appointments,
arrivals and departures, names and numbers.

On nights like these, which of us needs reminding
to set an eel-trap, open up the bomb doors
or sail out of the harbour on a spring tide?
What sway do you hold over our affairs?
Although for some you're all that's there, printed
across the white weeks until New Year;
moving towards windows that will not frame us,
into the evenings of our sons and daughters.

The Big Hum

(*sotto voce*)

I'm on the edge of a reed bed, just before dawn,
a slight breeze and a clear sky growing light.
That *chirruc* is a reed warbler close by.
As the birds grow active, I become stock-still

and part of the landscape, which lends my voice
that furtive veritas of cigarettes
across no-man's-land, Attenborough with the apes;
an intimacy with the baffled mic

in my small hours stakeout. Miles of tape
wind through the twilight, getting it all down.
You can hear a nightjar droning in the distance.
That booming bittern needs no introduction.

A black-headed gull going over seems to scold
that my half of the bed is growing cold.
That finger-down-a-comb's the corncrake's song.
And that's the water rail's sharming and trills.

These are my early ablutions, out of doors.
And you can close your eyes and open up
a great space, stitched by wrens and plumbed by larks
as light strengthens. That whirring sound's a snipe

beating its wings. Installed in ditch or hedge,
I've learned to keep the man-made at arm's length
from an early age, out on the city's edge,
my own unbroken voice the commentary

on the first tape I made: a C60
lowered in a machine by its mains cord
out of my bedroom window to record
sparrow clans of the nineteen-seventies

when birdsong had the streets all to itself
and even listening back now, there's that thrill
of timelessness: the shouts and breaking bottles
cooled to a dawn that's seen it all before.

But I don't romanticise the birds, like poets.
Their songs are strictly territorial,
perfumed and glandular, bitter as gall,
a media spend on advertising, or

their KEEP OUT signs, their re-election campaigns
sung to rivals up and down the food chain,
their contact calls, instant graffiti, bursts
declaring they've survived overnight frost.

My natural enemies are wind and rain,
a turbine coming over the earth's curve
that nobody can see but I can hear.
I keep away from roads and rush hours.

Still, even on mornings when I've found
a niche so isolate from rumble, hiss
or cattle; a spot that I could call my own
to the extent that you could score a radius

and say with some degree of certainty
I am the loneliest person in these Isles,
even beyond the high office of rain gauges
and transmitter masts, I’ve heard this sound:

I call it The Big Hum. I’ve heard it on
the stillest, most remote of nights. It seems
as if all this attentiveness to background
has teased me to a greater tuning in

and I can hear the room tone of the world
like an approaching storm. I blamed the blood
spiralling through my ears at first, but there
it was, picked up on tape. Others have tried

explaining it in terms of The Big Bang,
a vestige of which vibrates in the silence
of five-bar gates and stones. Then there are those
who understand eternal Sanskrit noise

to be the cause. I’m not having any of this.
From the damp and dead legs of the first position
of level meter and boom microphone,
I’ve heard the gain cranked up over the years.

And so I’ve made this tape for a winter evening
at home, when the only trace of birdsong
is a blackbird guttered down under a street lamp.
A tape in which I count the species in

out of my archive, into the studio's ark
before The Big Hum drowns them out. It starts
with a nightingale, deep in the broadleaved past
of a Kent beech wood in nineteen-eighty-six,

and then a heron from north Lancashire
on a cloudy morning in seventy-four;
a curlew from the Somerset Levels
fades in from seventy-seven, and then a dipper

sings counterpoint to the exact babble
of the Cumbrian streambed it lived beside;
a raven *kronks* from high over the fells
of three decades ago, and all the warblers

of Oxfordshire and Gloucestershire I've ever known
chime in, followed by lapwings taped in childhood
on a day I made a scarecrow wear a wire,
all built over tonight, and turned to stone;

I splice them all and dub them, one by one,
the wildfowl and the hawks, and take it right
out to the edges' kittiwakes and gannets
where the sea drinks up the analogue signal;

and have to shout over everything happening at once,
the whole island a bird colony, the song
and calls of forty springs to see me through
the dark winter ahead. Until I press STOP.

The Brick

They've finally come for me. The game is up
in the hour before dawn that steals back streetlight,
the dark soaked up by a rogue brick on a blind wall.
The neighbours have come out. They must have known
it couldn't last. And so I'm taken down.
Somebody must be writing product recalls
on all my books, proofreading through the night
to check I've gone, re-drawing all the maps.

It was good though, while it lasted. I hand it back
to classically trained specialists-in-their-fields,
the source-to-sea merchants, the moonrise freaks
and those who tell us animals are Other
over and over … O little brothers
and sisters, never blank that brick, nor speak
ill of the plain objects this dawn revealed!
We came this way. We too can leave some tracks.

The English Hit

The trains that tilt and the big landfills,
The towns all built round the simple thrills,
The whole thing caught in a movie of sorts
That they cut and put out on those nights we stay in.

The forty names you've got for the rain,
The No Ball Games and the blood in your veins,
The city in summer when the soul does a runner
And the dirty old bathwater has gone down the drain.

CHORUS
England, you did me and left me for dead,
One in the heart and one in the head.
You left me for dead, I was done from the start,
One in the head and one in the heart.

The season of mists when the leaves who enlist
Every spring think fuck this, and it's hard to resist
All the clocks going back and the plan of attack
Of winter, who has you and me on its Z-list.

The WI with the broadband and Wi-Fi,
The north-south divide and the mobile phone sci-fi,
The big private view you *really should get to*
And to *tell you the truth* that's *no word of a lie.*

CHORUS
England, you did me and left me for dead,
One in the heart and one in the head.
You left me for dead, I was done from the start,
One in the head and one in the heart.

Your awaydays, half closing days, dress-down-Fridays,
Seven eleven days, one-of-those-days days,
Dog days and rain-moving-in-from-the-west days,
Your fake-your-own-death-cos-I'm-so-fucking-bored days.

The girl at the cash-point, the Friday night flashpoint,
The no-return, nothing-to-smoke-but-the-ash point,
The daytrips and cream teas, the match on the big screen,
I just close my eyes and you seem like a dream.

CHORUS TO FADE

The English Hit (Doc Brown's Rap Version)

The trains that spill their loads on landfills
In towns still built round simple thrills
Let'em tempt you, give the underbelly a tickle
Tastes switch so quick, call us picky and fickle
But the experience is cinematic cameo in the Director's edit
Hoping that I might just make the credits
Or am I just another name?
Like another drop of rain in the drains, see this blood in my veins?
It's a second generational immigrant strain
No Blacks, no Irish and no ball games, but things change
My relationship is love/hate, just wait, as much as you inspire, you frustrate

CHORUS
My English Rose left me for dead,
One in the heart and one in the head but …
I suppose I shoulda known from the start,
One in the head and one in the heart
RPT

They say it's harmless, but for the benefit of six farmers
The clocks go back and we are trapped in the darkness
A season of mist descends, never ends
Days feel like cul-de-sacs and dead ends
Now I'm back on the booze again
Too dependent, maybe, lately, who's my friend?
I got 200 names saved in my phonebook and oh look –
There's no people I really want to speak to
Have I gone bad? When's my last time of eye contact?
I just text, email and the rest
Wi-Fi, why hide behind the sci-fi?

Online, I suppose, no North-South divide
No skin colour lines, no love at first sight
Wish spring would come by and bring the sunshine
Watching better lives advertised, televised like the truth
As if it's no word of a lie

CHORUS
My English Rose left me for dead,
One in the heart and one in the head but …
I suppose I shoulda known from the start,
One in the head and one in the heart

I'm full of grey Mondays, half closed Sundays
Quiet-when-you-cum days, Kids Club Fundays
Wear your church best days like your day-of-rest days
Cold fronts … moving in from the west days
Dog days, pea soup, muggy smog and fog days,
Odd days, "I don't wanna go into my job" days
More days, fake your own death coz you're bored days
All days come and go always
The girl at the cash point, the Friday night flashpoint
The no return, nothing to smoke but the ash point
Fat joints, cream teas, matches on the big screen,
Close my eyes so that you seem like a big dream …

CHORUS
My English Rose left me for dead,
One in the heart and one in the head but …
I suppose I shoulda known from the start,
One in the head and one in the heart

Thinking Shingle

Thinking shingle, from my muddy, alluvial bed,
from the bottle-necked Mersey and silted-up mouth of the Dee,
from a place where you just catch a strip of an olive-green beach
from a sea wall at low tide. Thinking shingle tonight
where the Ribble and Lune barely make it to open sea,
from Morecambe's mudflats, where there isn't no shingle in sight,
where there isn't no *sea* in sight, and girls in the bus shelters
are drinking Cinzano Bianco and missing shingle.

Thinking shingle, because shingle means Romantic other-
beaches, the clickers and hissers of Arnold,
the drinkers of seas, generators of authentic surf
sound effects, and a big hit with nuclear power stations.
Thinking the shingle spectrum at Chesil, from wren's egg
to Cox's Pippin, arranged by the tide's sorting office;
of Brighton's collection of steel combs from Mods and Rockers,
and the number crunching Ice Age flints of Dungeness
shining in moonlight. Its backwash sounds like radio:
ten thousand creative writing students have said so.

Longshore drift happens where there is shingle, not here
where waves fall at your feet without even so much
as a long, melancholy roar. Thinking shingle
with a mind of its own, with a back-suck, too big to fling up
at a guesthouse window in the dawn; the clean grey mean
where art might happen, tonight. Turn your radio off
and listen, right out to the edges, beyond the Big Hum,
and it's there, with the wind sharpening its knife: thinking shingle.

Afterword

In the years when I grew up there was no internet, but there was radio. Radio was a primitive world wide web: very surf-able, especially its shortwave bandwidths that teemed with strange time signals, warbling modulations, bursts of Arabic singing, Eastern European news bulletins and phrases of Morse code. You could argue it was better than the internet: the wireless seemed infinitely mysterious, and tweaking the illuminated dial lit with the names of distant places – Stockholm, Hilversum, Rome – took you on journeys. Mostly, I liked the voices. Even the ones I couldn't understand. And radio captivates us once we've acknowledged the paradox at its heart: the way we know many others must be listening, and yet a voice seems to be speaking out of the grainy silence to you and you alone.

All of the poems collected here were written for radio, but the initial terms of their tenure are quite various. For some of them, a phone call from an arts producer, or an email marked 'urgent', were the earliest overtures. I have even said 'yes' to a producer, only to get a call back an hour or two later telling me to 'stop writing', eventually receiving a small Disturbance Fee many months later for doing nothing but think about writing a poem. Others began more speculatively, but with a much longer lead in, and a surer sense of a theme around which an entire programme might be made. But in either case, the challenge has been the same: to write something that will work coming out of a speaker, as a spoken piece.

As well as starting out under different circumstances, the poems found themselves framed differently on air. Some were cued in by the presenter in a dead studio, others were presented onstage before a live audience. Some were recorded out in the world and edited together to form a sequence, others used radiophonic effects and textures, creating montage. One was phoned in to Broadcasting House from a call box at 'the exact geographical centre of Great Britain'. Sometimes I was invited to say a few exculpatory words about what I'd tried to do, and sometimes my fellow guests in the studio were encouraged to respond at the end. A few were left hanging in the ether, followed by Greenwich pips or the Continuity Announcer.

Over the years, I grew fond of this folder of poems that didn't seem to fit anywhere else (only four of the poems published here have made it into my other collections). But fond enough to publish them? On balance, yes. They seem to belong together: partners in crime, but related in all kinds of other ways, too. Over time, often working with the same producers, we began to make little discoveries that hopefully were carried over and developed from project to project. Themes recurred, often running athwart the main business at hand. I also discovered that I'm always thinking about the page, even when I'm writing for the ear: if the poem didn't possess any formal pressure, or a shapeliness the eye could also register, then I noticed the appeal of reading it into a microphone diminished. The big decision so far as I was concerned has been to leave this work unedited after broadcast. What you have here are the poems as they went out.

If I've found people sometimes critical of commissioned writing, it's usually along the lines of 'the muse will not be bribed'. I've also wondered whether producing a poem for an arts magazine show co-opts creativity into the dismal world of brief and deadline and outcome. But my worries have always been outweighed by one simple fact: as for film and theatre, you will never do anything more collaborative, as a writer, than make a piece of work for broadcast. The medium is intrinsically collaborative. The deadline isn't inimical to poetry either: we're all working towards one. Ideally, a commission takes you out of yourself and, if you're lucky, deposits you right back in the middle of all those things your imagination cares most about; that nourishing place you can't always easily get to by waiting for lyric inspiration to arrive at your desk.

I've always admired those writers who've managed to achieve the occasional and civic poem, especially those who've tried to produce work for a wider audience using a newer medium, as well as more lyric or intimate work. Auden at the GPO Film Unit. Tony Harrison and the team of directors, editors and composers he worked with making his film/poems. Radio – in many ways a superb medium for poetry – is so much more fleeting than film or even television, and after a few years of writing for it, even with the advent of podcasting, I began to wonder about the afterlife of broadcast poems. Maybe this is why a gathering in print felt more and more viable.

In the end, I've come to view this work – and maybe this is true of all commissioned poetry – as being circumscribed by a tension between disposability and durability, between the immediate, the task-in-hand, and the infinitely resonant, the long player. How many of these poems manage to slip free of radio's evanescent world of stop-watched seconds and minutes, and transmit something to the reader in metrical time, on the printed page, I couldn't possibly say. Beyond foolishly trying to predict what will ever happen to any piece of writing, only one thing is for certain: when our sun has swollen and the planet can no longer support any life, when all human language, and the idea of language itself, has been lost, and our books and servers are dust, these ephemeral, written-to-order, occasional poems will continue travelling as electromagnetic waves through the dark and silence of deep space, audible in our neighbouring galaxies – in amongst all the shipping forecasts, Top 40s and serenaded nightingales – should there be anyone there to hear them.

Notes

The Sorting Office

Broadcast: 20th December 1998
Producer: Rob Ketteridge

Programme: Open Book
Channel: BBC Radio 4

My first ever radio commission. The programme had some kind of a chilly, wintry theme that I was meant to loosely address (the other guests were Valentine Cunningham, Richard Davenport-Hines and Francis Spufford, who'd just published his Antarctica book *I May Be Some Time*), and it was Christmastime, but beyond this all I can say is that the 'postman albatross' was lifted from *Moby Dick*, and Melville's long footnote to 'The Whiteness of the Whale'; and I'd heard of seasonal temps at sorting offices – possibly apocryphal, this – having to burn children's letters addressed to Santa's grotto. The late Humphrey Carpenter was the presenter.

Chalk: an Epistle

Broadcast: 16th June 2005
Producers: Allegra McIlroy/Kirsty Pope

Programme: Night Waves
Channel: BBC Radio 3

The Tate had launched their exhibition *A Picture of Britain*, and this commission, given to myself and four other writers, was an invitation to address some feature of the British landscape significant or important to us.

North Atlantic Corridor

Broadcast: 19th February 1999
Producers: Rob Ketteridge

Programme: Front Row
Channel: BBC Radio 4

This was a real 'short order' commission, as Front Row's often were. I got a call asking me if I'd like to write something that celebrated the anniversary of the first ever in-flight movie being shown, and only had days to come up with something.

The Spindle

Broadcast: 28th September 2007
Producer: Zahid Warley

Programme: The Verb
Channel: BBC Radio 3

A few years before this commission, I'd made another programme with Zahid and had mentioned to him how I'd just visited the exact geographical centre of the British Isles, near a village in the

Forest of Bowland called Dunsop Bridge: real Tolkein, Middle Earth country (actually, this claim is inconveniently disputed, but that's another story). The site is marked by a telephone booth. Being a producer, he earmarked this and eventually asked me if I could write something about it, and what's more, could I phone it in to Broadcasting House from the geographical centre while the show was being recorded live? Of course I said yes. So I was stood in a phone box in the middle of nowhere, the dead centre, talking to Ian McMillan and his audience in the BBC Radio Theatre on the other end of a crackly line, wondering how I'd be able to claim back the slummy I was feeding into the coin slot.

The Sound of Music

Broadcast: 4th August 2000
Producer: Rob Ketteridge

Programme: Front Row
Channel: BBC Radio 4

This came about because of a 'soundtrack to summer' theme being featured on Front Row, and around the same time I'd visited Tate Liverpool and had seen an installation by Douglas Gordon called *Something between my mouth and your ear*, which in turn put me in mind of a family story, and the poem got going from there.

Ports

Broadcast: 5th March 2005
Producer: Emma Harding

Programme: Between the Ears
Channel: BBC Radio 3

I'd wanted to write a radio poem that linked three ports – one of antiquity, one in the process of re-inventing itself, and one modern and thriving – across time and space, and got the chance through a commission for Between the Ears. I'd originally looked at Tyre being the ancient port, but then Carthage emerged as a much better option; the others would be Liverpool and Rotterdam. The poem was experimental in that, beyond the loose sense outlined above, I had no idea how I would make the ports 'talk' until I visited them. So much of this was written on the move, or in situ: most of the first section and envoi was worked out in the actual ruins of Carthage, or at Sidi Bou Said; the Rotterdam section was mainly written in my room in the Maritime Hotel, overlooking the Nieuwe Maas: the list of barges' names at the end was taken from what container traffic passed by my window one afternoon. The producer Emma Harding spent hours collecting the kinds of local sounds needed for texture and atmosphere, and then the programme was assembled back in London.

For St Jerome

Broadcast: 14th February 2000
Producer: Rob Ketteridge

Programme: Front Row
Channel: BBC Radio 4

Front Row wanted a poem that marked the anniversary of the opening of the first public libraries, so far as I can recall, and it was going out on St Valentine's Day, so could I, somehow, weave these two elements together?

An Erratic

Broadcast: 24th December 2001
Producer: Rob Ketteridge

Programme: Front Row
Channel: BBC Radio 4

After George Harrison died, I got a call asking me if I'd like to write something, and I'd already started this. The railed-off glacial boulder outside Wavertree Library in Liverpool is well known in that part of the city, but everybody – myself and George Harrison included – grew up thinking it was from outer space.

Blind Scouse

Broadcast: 10th December 2008
Producer: Ekene Akalawu

Programme: Front Row
Channel: BBC Radio 4

I was invited to take part in a Front Row special looking back at Liverpool's Capital of Culture year, which was recorded before an audience in the city. I was asked to write anything on the way Liverpool might have changed in recent times; indeed, has always been a work-in-progress, taking a cue from the mid-nineteenth-century street ballad 'Liverpool's An Altered Town', though I seem to have drifted towards an idea of 'scouse' as a word where the culinary, linguistic and the cultural intersect; as a thing that might bind a place together.

In Liftless Country

Broadcast: 23rd February 2003
Producer: Sue Roberts

Programme: Word on the Street
Channel: BBC Radio 4

Movers and Shakers

Broadcast: 23rd February 2003
Producer: Sue Roberts

Programme: Word on the Street
Channel: BBC Radio 4

Shitemere

Broadcast: 23rd February 2003
Producer: Sue Roberts

Programme: Word on the Street
Channel: BBC Radio 4

I think this was the first Word on the Street programme (it ran for quite some time), with Jackie Kay presenting; I'd been asked to write about being in residence at Dove Cottage and the Wordsworth Trust, and the Lake District generally.

Civic

Broadcast: 18th February 2003
Producer: Tim Dee

Programme: Afternoon Poem
Channel: BBC Radio 4

This was my part of a commission given to five poets: to write on a watery theme. When I'd lived in Grasmere the Thirlmere reservoir water passed quite close to my house, on its way to Manchester. At the time of this commission I'd just discovered a huge pipe passing over the River Lune, a Victorian aquaduct, near my new home in Lancaster; this was the same supply, a little closer to its destination now. So I'd already been thinking about this for some time when the offer came in. Tim insisted we go up to Thirlmere to record, so what went out was the poem issuing from its imaginative and actual source, the banks of the reservoir. Tim's attention to detail extended to the musical treatment: it had to be Walton's *Belshazzar's Feast*, performed by the Hallé Orchestra ('By the waters of Babylon …'); it had to be The Fall doing 'Pay Your Rates' ('pay your water-rates!').

She Wandered

Broadcast: 19th February 2006
Producer: Zahid Warley

Programme: The Verb
Channel: BBC Radio 3

The Verb wanted a poem for a seasonal programme featuring Wordsworth's famous 'I wandered lonely as a cloud …' lyric. When I was a kid, older people had always impressed me by being able to recite this poem, and others, having learned them by rote at school when they were children, so the resultant poem's concerned with memory and memorizing as much as anything else.

A Stranger's Guide

Broadcast: 28th October 2001
Producer: Tim Dee

Programme: Fast Fish and Loose Fish
Channel: BBC Radio 4

This was a programme marking the 150th anniversary of Melville's *Moby Dick*, a very welcome commission, as this has always been an important book for me. When I was younger I was also taken with his earlier novel *Redburn*, which imagines a journey to Liverpool (which Melville had made), and the eponymous cabin-boy hero trying to find his way around the city using his father's old guidebook, which proved difficult. I'd already touched on this elsewhere, but here imagine Melville (jnr) jumping ship on that earlier voyage.

Synchronous Lateral Excitation

Broadcast: 25th February 2002
Producer: Julian May

Programme: Night Waves
Channel: BBC Radio 3

I got a call from a fellow poet, the late and much-missed Michael Donaghy, who had accepted a commission for a poem celebrating the reopening of the Millennium Bridge over the Thames. The structure had developed the wobble of a Tarzan vine ladder, and Michael was trying to conflate this with a human sense of falling into rhythm and step that chimed with some of his own ideas about form and poetry: but he'd hit a wall. What we ended up doing was meeting each other halfway and co-writing it, so that every other line was originally written in rhyming couplets, then interleaved. Neither of us thought this was our finest hour ('our very own Tay Bridge disaster') and tried to forget about it, so imagine our surprise when the London Sinfonietta called to ask permission to use it as part of a performance. I'm told Maureen Lipman and Tom Courtenay co-read this at the Queen Elizabeth Hall.

July (Wedding Haiku)

Broadcaster: 16th November 2007
Producer: Nicola Holloway

Programme: The Verb
Channel: BBC Radio 3

As ephemeral as it gets: I got a call just a few hours before going to the studio about the possibility of producing a haiku for the programme, and wrote this on the back of an envelope in the hotel. It's an image I've had knocking around for years, looking for a home and not previously finding one.

The Great Violinski

Broadcast: 30th August 2000
Producer: Fiona McLean

Programme: Poetry Proms
Channel: BBC Radio 3

This was written for the first Poetry Proms, alongside other new work broadcast during intervals during the BBC Proms 2000. I was 'in residence' up at the Wordsworth Trust at this time, and remembered a school visit to Dove Cottage where a teenage boy waved me conspiratorially to one side, and asked me, straight-faced, whether there really had been a Wordsworth. I was taken aback: what did he think this all was? And then he said to me: 'But that name *Wordsworth* … For a *writer*. It's like saying there's a famous composer called Violinski.' So this notional character was already alive to me before I got asked to do this.

World of Sport

Broadcast: 4th July 2006
Producer: Zahid Warley

Programme: Night Waves
Channel: BBC Radio 3

Diary Moon

Broadcast: 16th May 2001
Producer: Clare Holland

Programme: Night Waves
Channel: BBC Radio 3

A lunar theme from Night Waves. I could have been thinking of Elizabeth Bishop's 'Sestina', and her almanac, as much as my Liverpool Taxicab Trade's Blind Children's Fund Diary.

The Big Hum

Broadcast: 8th December 2004
Producer: Tim Dee

Programme: Rebuilding the Ark
Channel: BBC Radio 3

I'm a fan of field recordings – I'm the kind of person who gets excited by finding something like *A Sound Guide to the Grasshoppers and Crickets of Western Europe* by Ragge and Reynolds, or collections of the calls of newspaper vendors – but I especially like those of birds, and have been collecting them for some time. I've noticed the way the human interjections in early recordings – the moment a voice will identify what you're hearing – are very stark and patrician; just this sudden, enunciated 'WOOD WARBLER', whereas more recently they've gotten quite naturalistic themselves. So somebody like Geoff Sample will cozy himself down in the undergrowth and tell you about it, describing the weather and conditions too, before identifying the birds quite casually, and even mimicking them himself for the listener. And they *are* an odd breed: men (usually men) who rise in the pre-dawn dark to lug cables and parabolic mikes for miles into the landscape. So I had this voice, the voice of a field recorder, in my head for years. When I got asked to contribute to Rebuilding the Ark, which was a whole evening of wildlife programming on Radio 3, I thought of this voice, and also of the 'big hum' I'd heard about as a kid; the impossibility, even in our remotest countryside, of total silence.

The Brick

Broadcast: 7th September 2008
Producer: Aasiya Lodhi
Programme: The Lament of Swordy Well
Channel: BBC Radio 4

This short lyric was written for an arts feature on John Clare, and specifically his 'Swordy Well' poems of place.

The English Hit

Broadcast: 6th January 2008
Producer: Ella-Mai Robey
Programme: A Poet's Song
Channel: BBC Radio 4

The English Hit (Doc Brown's Rap Version)

Broadcast: 6th January 2008
Producer: Ella-Mai Robey
Programme: A Poet's Song
Channel: BBC Radio 4

There's been a staple, journalistic shit-stirring question doing the rounds for years: who was better, Keats or Dylan? This programme presented what actually happened when a couple of poets were charged with writing a serviceable song lyric for a recording artist. Jo Shapcott was paired up with Jamie Cullum, and I was asked to write something for a rapper, Doc Brown. The two versions of 'The English Hit' here are the version I worked on and handed over to Doc as 'finished', and then the version he actually used to rap from in the studio.

Thinking Shingle

Broadcast: 1st November 2003
Producer: Zahid Warley

Programme: The Verb
Channel: BBC Radio 3

I don't remember how this came about, except that it was eventually recorded live in front of an audience at the Aldeburgh Poetry Festival in 2003, where I do remember being sat onstage between the late Gael Turnbull, Paul Durcan and Daljit Nagra. All of a sudden, as I was reading the poem, the white noise of surf and the hiss of backwash filled the hall. The night before, the producer and I had gone down to the beach to record some authentic shingle to give some texture to the broadcast. It was freezing cold, and the incoming waves caught us unawares on a few crunchy retreats (drink had been taken) and soaked us. We could have pulled it up from the sound archive – where they probably have not only 'shingle beach' but 'shingle beach: Aldeburgh: November' – but then I wouldn't have this abiding memory of laughing in the pitch dark with a man trying to steady a big fluffy microphone pointed out to sea in a howling gale.

Also available from Donut Press

Caligula on Ice and Other Poems, by Tim Turnbull.
£10

Rougher Yet, by Tim Wells.
£10

Boys' Night Out in the Afternoon, by Tim Wells.
£10

Stranded in Sub-Atomica, by Tim Turnbull.
£10

Approaches To How They Behave, by W.S. Graham.
£5

The Adventures of Monsieur Robinet, by John Hegley.
£5

Frankie, Alfredo,, by Liane Strauss.
£5

The Observations of Alexandr Svetlov, by Colette Bryce.
£5

Super Try Again, by Roddy Lumsden.
£5

A Voids Officer Achieves the Tree Pose, by Annie Freud.
£5

The Glutton's Daughter, by Sinéad Wilson.
£5

www.donutpress.co.uk